How Things Grow

From Seed
to Dandelion

By Jan Kottke

Children's Press
A Division of Grolier Publishing
New York / London / Hong Kong / Sydney
Danbury, Connecticut

Photo Credits: Cover and all photos © Dwight Kuhn

Contributing Editors: Mark Beyer and Eliza Berkowitz
Book Design: MaryJane Wojciechowski

Visit Children's Press on the Internet at:
http://publishing.grolier.com

Library of Congress Cataloging-in-Publication Data

Kottke, Jan.
    From seed to dandelion / by Jan Kottke.
      p. cm. — (How things grow)
    Includes bibliographical references and index.
    Summary: Simple text and photographs show how a seed becomes a dandelion.
    ISBN 0-516-23310-6 (lib. bdg.) — ISBN 0-516-23510-9 (pbk.)
    1. Common dandelion—Life cycles—Juvenile literature. 2. Seeds—Dispersal—Juvenile
literature. [1.Dandelions. 2. Seeds—Dispersal.] I. Title.

QK495.C74 K68 2000
583'.99—dc21

                                                                      00-024368

0 1021 0138574 2

Contents

1 Dandelion Seeds   4

2 Dandelions Grow   10

3 Dandelions Everywhere   16

4 New Words   22

5 To Find Out More   23

6 Index   24

7 About the Author   24

These are **dandelion** puff balls.

Puff balls are made of dandelion **seeds**.

5

The seeds fall off the **stem**.

The seeds are blown by the wind.

7

The wind carries the seeds.

They will make more dandelions.

9

A seed lands in **soil**.

A new plant is growing from the seed.

11

The dandelion flowers begin to **bloom**.

They have green leaves all around them.

Dandelions grow all over.

They grow wherever the seeds land.

15

A lot of seeds landed in this field.

Now it is covered with dandelion flowers.

17

These are full-grown dandelions.

Dandelion flowers have many **petals**.

19

Bees bring **pollen** to dandelion flowers.

Pollen helps dandelions to make seeds.

More dandelions will grow from these seeds.

21

New Words

bloom (**bloom**) to become a flower

dandelion (**dan**-dee-leyen) a flower with yellow petals

petals (**peh**-tuhlz) a part of a flower

pollen (**pah**-len) a powder that helps flowers make seeds

seeds (**seedz**) the small parts of plants that grow into new plants

soil (**soyl**) dirt

stem (**stem**) thin part of a plant that grows from the ground

To Find Out More

Books

A Dandelion's Life
by John Himmelman
Children's Press

Dandelions
by Kathleen V. Kudlinski
The Lerner Publishing Group

Dandelion
by Barry Watts
Silver Burdett Press

The Dandelion Seed
by Joseph A. Anthony
Dawn Publications

Web Sites

The Dandelion
www.cyberfair.org/ntrail/ntweb1/ndandeli.html
Learn more about dandelions, including what they look like and when they grow.

What is a Flower?
http://tqjunior.advanced.org/3715/flower.html
This site tells the story of flowers and how plants grow.

Index

bees, 20
bloom, 12

dandelion(s), 4, 8, 12, 14, 16, 18, 20

flowers, 12, 16, 18

petals, 18
pollen, 20
puff balls, 4

seed(s), 4, 6, 8, 10, 14, 16, 20
soil, 10

stem, 6
wind, 6, 8

About the Author

Jan Kottke is the owner/director of several preschools in the Tidewater area of Virginia. A lifelong early education professional, she is completing a phonics reading series for preschoolers.

Reading Consultants

Kris Flynn, Coordinator, Small School District Literacy, The San Diego County Office of Education

Shelly Forys, Certified Reading Recovery Specialist, W.J. Zahnow Elementary School, Waterloo, IL

Peggy McNamara, Professor, Bank Street College of Education, Reading and Literacy Program